MW01242932

Real
ANSWERS

Real
AUTHORS

60 Marketing Tips from
Self-Published Authors
and Publishers.

Jill Mettendorf

Real Answers from Real Authors
60 Marketing Tips from
Self-Published Authors and Publishers

ISBN-10: 0-9895793-0-1
ISBN-13: 978-1-61813-083-9

To request a consultation or information on services:
866-341-9588
jill@mirabooksmart.com
www.realanswersrealauthors.com

Printed in the United States of America

Mira Publishing,
a Division of Graphic Connections Group
174 Chesterfield Industrial Blvd.
Chesterfield, MO 63005

Book Design by: Jill Mettendorf
Editing by: Anne O'Brien

First Edition: August 2013
Second Printing: November 2014

To all of my authors…

Thank you for giving me the opportunity to help you. Not only have I learned from your expertise but I have had a chance to grow and appreciate the art of a self-published book.

1 | Honest Lewis
Parasites

Know your market. My market is a bit strange - I sell books at tattoo conventions, nightclubs, and tattoo shops. My market is basically men who have tattoos on their neck, ride motorcycles, and have beards. Also, I host open mic nights. Spoken word, poetry, hip-hop, freestyle, singer-songwriter, ranting, stand-up comedy. I'm really enabled in this because I'm in Nashville, Tennessee, and it's a city that's very conducive towards arts, music, and writing. I'm also involved in the Nashville art scene. People read my books and spoken word pieces at their gallery shows.

The best thing I think you can do as a writer is meet people who read books. Meet strangers, let them know what you do, and that you're passionate about it. I've never met an author whose book I didn't purchase. Also, I've made contacts with all the indie bookstores in the Tennessee area and we have arrangements to sell through them. They're not very profitable - basically it covers production and transport costs - but it gets us read, and it gets us on bookshelves.

Meet people. Meet everyone. Find a microphone and talk into it. Let the world know that you stand behind your art. I've had at least one speaking engagement every week for the past six months. Lots of people and lots of venues. Some empty. Some with a hundred people. You can't be discouraged by a 'slow' reception. Know that you're building something. And that it takes time.

2 | Mary Douglas

*Clement Chronicles: Guide to Genealogical &
Historical Research in Kansas; Salina's Historic
Downtown*
www.historicalmatters.com

Target your marketing to your intended audience! I took pre-order forms to the annual meeting of the Kansas Genealogical Society and had a librarian colleague post a notice about my book to a librarians-only mail list. I also sent pre-order forms to the Kansas State Historical Society Center for Historical Research. The original run of 300 copies sold out in less than a year. And I'm still getting requests from out of state librarians.

Marketing is a very expensive endeavor. If funds are limited I would urge any new author to take advantage of all free marketing tools, such as Twitter, Facebook, Linkedin, and many of the other social networking sites out there. They are free and maintaining a presence on each and or all of them can't be a bad idea. Take advantage of any speaking opportunities. Is the book ~~is~~ religious in nature, or about safety or something positive? Most churches will open their door for a brief speech on the issue. If there is any money available for use, a website with a PayPal button is also a good source of promotion. All you need to do then is drive people to the website. If possible, shoot a short promotional video on the book and make copies on CDs to distribute. The making of the video may be a bit pricey, but copying it to CD is not very expensive and in most cases you can do this yourself. Entry of the book in some book fairs may be a good idea if you feel the target audience will attend that fair. For a small fee, most books can be entered.

*Police and Fire Publishing – Reality Based Law
Enforcement Books*
www.policeandfirepublishing.com

You have to believe in yourself and your book(s). There will be ridicule and opposition to your success. Most great people faced this when they started. Ignore the haters and move on.

Utilize your connections to speak to groups, and that means any group. You are now the expert. Everyone in the world talks about writing a book, but very few do...and even fewer write a quality book. There will always be people who scoff and say they know more than you. I have come up with a one-liner for them: "Write your own book."

Resist the urge to give away your book for free! Most people will pay, but a few will act like they deserve a comp. They don't! You sat at the computer for thousands of hours and they won't shell out 20 bucks. A great one-liner to break the awkwardness is, "When you write yours I promise to buy two copies!" The only person who deserves a comp is your mother!

actually not the point.

Social media is great, but make no mistake about it, the best method of sales is personal contact, and that means seminars with a display of your products. Get a Square credit card reader for your smartphone; most people pay with credit cards these days.

Place a sign on your table that says 'Great gift idea' and the price of your book. I have found if you place the amount in plain view, sales are better. I know if I don't see a price I will not approach. Encourage the lookie loos to pick up the book (studies show a significant increase in purchases when an individual actually touches the product).

5 | George Warren
Starr Light in the Christmas Story; Hope in a Hurried World; Emily the Ant

There are a host of helpful services you can purchase or ideas for marketing online. However, I personally think there are two key factors. First, make your book known by public appearances. I attend events at which books can be sold (town festivals, Christmas pageants, flea markets, etc.). I have also approached retail stores that might carry local authors (craft stores, independent bookstores, even libraries by giving part of the proceeds to the library, etc.). The second key factor is having a website to point people to where they can purchase your books.

One tip is to go to conferences and use your book as the basis for your presentation, and the other is to use your book as a workshop text. I did this and as a result I sold most of my books and was seen by a major publisher who just published my book in a much expanded form.

7 | Katrinka Moore
Brevitas Anthology

Our Brevitas group always holds a reading (we call it a festival) to celebrate our poetry and the annual anthology. People who come to the reading pay a small fee and get a copy of the book.

For books of poetry of my own that I've had published, I always set up readings with different poets to celebrate the publication of my book. That way I get audience members who may not know me and hopefully some of them will buy the book. I keep copies on hand to take to any readings I'm involved in.

Many writers maintain a blog and use that to help promote the book. The blog would include a link to the Mira store so readers could buy the book.

Nonfiction authors can look to local media to try to get an article or an interview on the subject of their book. For instance, for a nonfiction book on sports safety the author can be interviewed and provide tips for listeners/readers, getting them interested enough to buy the book.

So I think readings (and signing the books), blogging, and connecting with local media are ways authors can promote their books.

8 | Michael Herr

The Old Queen and the Maui Maiden; Bones of the Kuhina Nui

Create a Facebook page for your book. Speak (for free) to local groups. I maintain a database of people who have bought my books, and send them info (postcards) whenever I publish a new book. Get the local papers to do a story on you and your work.

9 | A.R. Silverberry
Wyndano's Cloak
www.arsilverberry.com

I tried a lot of things over the last three years. Hands down the most successful was live book signings. I wrote two blog articles on how I did it. Here are the links:

Art of the Meet and Greet Part 1: http://www.arsilverberry.com/art-of-the-meet-and-greet-part-i

Art of the Meet and Greet Part 2: http://indiewriterszone.blogspot.com/search?q=art+of+the+meet+and+greet

Design and Construction of Tube Guitar Amplifiers
www.translucidamps.com

I have a website that accepts credit cards. The book is for sale on eBay. I joined Amazon Advantage. I contacted many music stores and musical equipment web sites, and two or three agreed to stock my book. Note that the wholesale channels buy from me for 50%. I advertise every month in Guitar Player and Vintage Guitar magazine's classified ads. I believe this is the most important marketing tool (but it's expensive).

Because I have several books in the works, I had to hire a publicist. *LIFE minus 3 ½* was turned down by 62 literary agents without any of them looking at one page, so I went the self-publishing route. Because of the subject matter of my book, my publicist is sending out e-blasts to all sports columnists in my area along with anyone connected with compulsive gambling or self-help. I am also selling it on Amazon.

Create a Facebook page for the book. Invite everyone you can to "like" the page. Encourage friends and colleagues to purchase the book on the first day it appears on Amazon.com (this will boost its rating on Amazon). Arrange to be a speaker wherever you can (local Rotary clubs, national conferences, etc.) and have books for sale at the end of the event. Send gift books to people who will review/blog/publish their response to the book. Do a book signing event at local book stores.

Consider an eBook as well as the hard copy of the book, so that you can attract a larger group of readers.

13 | Don MacLean
Someday Honey
www.mirasmartshop.com

     I did a "meet the author" event and a book signing event with a couple of book stores, and split the sale proceeds 60/30 and 70/30, respectively. I also did an interview with a newspaper reporter which was published in the paper. I was also successful at a book fair. I also put out the word through email and Facebook. These were in addition to business cards I printed up and handed out to almost everyone I met. The cards indicate the book is available at www.mirasmartshop.com, my email address: somedayhoney@yahoo.com or by calling my phone number.

14 | Kevin D. Raphael Fitch
Celestial Configurations of Africa and the Caribbean
www.theastrologyconsultant.com

I recommend they read *The Well-Fed Self-Publisher* by Peter Bowerman. This book will provide the required tools to get their books sold.

A website is key, whereby they can sell their book online if they like, and also promote their book. They must have a presence on the web.

If they already have the eBook version of the book, they can check out BookLocker (booklocker.com). They will sell the eBook for them, through a non-exclusive contract, which means that they will not own the rights to their book. They have connections to Ingram, Amazon, Barnes and Noble, etc. They will get a percentage of each sale and send you a monthly commission check.

PRWEB is a good way to get exposure (prweb.com). They are a press release distribution business. An author should write a good press release to create a lot of buzz about the book.

15 | Forrest Canutt
Shame; All about Janet
www.amazon.com

One tip is to go to the main library where you live and surrounding communities and tell them you are a local author and would like to sell your book to the library system (could be a lot of books and also get exposure to readers). Next, you should hook up your authors with www.SavvyBookMarketer.com. They have some free downloads, a monthly newsletter, and a lot of great tips to market your book. These are the 2 ideas I have to begin with.

Start a blog (WordPress), and get some active content in it to attract attention. Get a kickstarter bid going to raise money to hire an actual PR agency. I'm also trying to get some air time with a radio program or two.

17 | Chris Michael Orndoff
The Blueseph J. Headmetal Saga
www.headmetalcomics.com

First, the world of Comics is vastly different than what I imagine it would be like for a novelist. The one BIG reason is that the Comic World has the Comic Convention, which is constantly growing in size and popularity. If you write Sci-Fi, Fantasy or Horror, I would highly recommend the Comic Convention avenue. Perhaps there is a "prose" convention scene out there that I'm unaware of, but without a doubt, the Comic Convention scene is a MUST for anyone trying to make a name in Comics/Fantasy/Sci-Fi/Horror.

Secondly, do not even attempt to get people to financially invest in your product if YOU have not yet financially invested in it. While we have not yet "broken-in" to the world of Comics, every step in the right direction has been made because I saved my own money to invest in myself first. I have been able to bring in industry professionals to work on my project for a few reasons, but none more important than the fact that when I approached these professional people, I spoke the language of CASH. I had to sell them on my work, and give them samples of my writing to prove to them that I was serious, but the bottom line for a professional is always money. Again, this advice may be more specific to Comics because you often see new Comic writers trying to pitch scripts to publishers, but Comic publishers want to see Sequential Art AND the Script.

To make this advice applicable to a novelist, I would say: If you are really serious about your book, then hire an artist to create a beautiful cover and then go to Mira and print at least 50 copies of a professional quality Hardcover to use for your pitch. Then, if you're going get a table at a convention, invest more money in making your display look good, e.g. banners, posters and other small merchandise.

Finally, take advantage of EVERY aspect of Social Media. I treat Facebook like it is a real place—yes, I know that sounds weird. I literally try to build real friendships with industry professionals. It is rather tricky to do that because these professionals have SO many fans and SO many of them are overbearing and constantly barraging them for advice without ever even attempting to treat them like people. Almost every professional contact I have made has been through Facebook, and those relationships have blossomed over a period of several months—if not years— of respect and admiration. I have turned Facebook friendships into working partnerships, and in some cases, without ever having to ask these people things like "Will you like my page?" or "Will you share my work?" I have been able to get very talented people to do just that.

*Grand Fences and Gates of the James J. Hill House;
Summit Avenue Coloring Book; Cathedral of Saint
Paul Coloring Book; Glensheen: The Historic Congdon
Estate Coloring Book; Minnesota North Shore Coloring
Book; Twin Cities Coloring Book; Summit Avenue
Mansions*
www. sorusbooks.webs.com

Marketing is hard work. Rapport with your clients is huge. I have 30 locations selling our books and I have a great relationship with all of them. Since most of our books have to do with history, I have held book talks at the Hill House. I know all of the tour guides and treat them like family because they are the people who will help sell my book.

Book talks or book signings will bring out the people. I am constantly meeting with store owners to get their thoughts on the books and to see what customers are interested in. When they had a home tour down in St. Paul we contacted the committee to see if we could sell our books in one of the mansions, and we were able to set up a stand and sell our books for a fee. That was all about getting our information out there. We handed out brochures and business cards.

Building a Website is another way to get your information out there. Put your books on it and all the locations that are selling the books. Going where events are being held is the best way to get your information out there.

If you are not comfortable with meeting and talking to people, you are in the wrong business. Marketing is hard work and it is not cheap. It can be very frustrating!

Having a great relationship with the bookstore owner or manager is the best advice that I can give because they are the ones selling your book.

19 | Jennifer Salmassian Khodadi
Happy Halloween Birthday Boy; Javakhk
www.amazon.com

I don't have the power the big publishers have, but I have a one-to-one approach that I give to my clients. For example, I call local schools and speak to librarians or academic directors. We arrange a day for a book read, then I leave fliers for purchase orders and sell the books with an autograph. I donate ~~back~~ to the school 20-30% so we both win. This is my #1 way of marketing. Tell any new author that they will have to have a certain quantity to give away.

I know that public librarians do have authority to purchase books, but by the time that happens, you may as well hand them a free copy. They also have library hours and will likely have you come back for a read aloud. You just have to make nice and hope people will support you.

You can write a press release to local papers, but the likelihood of taking off with that story is slim, unless you live in a very small town and not too much goes down in your area.

I have taken booths at arts/crafts festivals and book fairs. That is the worst, in my opinion. Tables cost big money and people want free stuff. They will pay for food and drinks but not books.

20 | Leslie Kim
123 Main Street…the Scamming of America
www.amazon.com

I'm an Editor/Publisher/Journalist, albeit one who works in the professional magazine field. Still, I get many friends, professional contacts and even "he's the brother-in-law of the guy who does the maintenance on my aunt's neighbor's '63 Porsche" approaching me for help on books.

The difference is that many of them find me prior to the actual publication (still in the editing process), and that's where I give them (what I consider to be) the best advice. The process of marketing the book needs to correctly start to coincide with the process of writing the book.

What's that mean?
Well, since in my humble opinion the first commandment of saleable writing is "Know Thy Audience," it's this exact stage of the game where we most need to <u>expand</u> our eventual marketing audience with an additional character, a sideline expertise, or mention of real geography (in a populated area). Me? I'll buy/read a book because it backgrounds in Detroit, Las Vegas or Orange County -- all places I know well because I've lived there. Throughout the writing process, there are ongoing opportunities to grab a larger chunk of audience.

Once it's published …
•   Social media is amazing and getting more amazing every day.

- Speaking gigs (but ONLY if you're a decent speaker)
- Local clubs, Retirement communities or Senior Living Centers
- Group insurers (Humana, United Health, etc. that have recreation halls for their members)
- Enrichment Lecturer series for multiple of the cruise lines. (Yes, the speaker can autograph/sell books immediately after a lecture ... and those sales add up.)

21 | Michael Gray, CPA

Secrets of Tax Planning for Employee Stock Options;
Employee Stock Options: Executive Tax Planning;
How to Use Roth & IRA Accounts; The Real Estate Tax
Handbook
www.taxtrimmers.com

My best advice is to promote to your list. If you have a newsletter or savings club list, promote your book to your subscribers. If you don't already have a list, create one. And create a list of the names and addresses of people who order your book directly--then promote your next book on the same topic to them.

My boss also promotes his books whenever he speaks to a group. This is a great way to sell books, if you don't mind public speaking and/or you are already doing it.

I also use Radio and TV Interview Report to promote media interviews. Their website is www.rtir.com.

I never thought that I would sell any books, but I'm on my fourth 100 book order, so here goes...

Create a Facebook page with a title that makes your page findable. Easy to do. Promote the book on your page. Add material and "posts" to your web page once a month or so.

Find other people's pages, and then post things with your signature, so anyone looking at that person's webpage will see your post and can click through to your webpage. This takes some ingenuity, time and effort.

Spend a few hundred dollars with PRWeb, an online company that puts out press releases to newspapers, etc., related to the topic of the book.

Create a webpage with the title of the book, and sell the book online or direct them to Amazon. There are many very low-cost website creating places you can go to (Google, GoDaddy, etc.) and lots of others. If this doesn't work, you can always cancel after a few years and not have spent a lot of money.

Create a business card for the book. Always leave some of these cards wherever you go, e.g., bank counters, professional offices, church areas, with all your friends, everywhere that will not be considered to be obnoxious.

Find online "blogs" (there are many directories) that are related to the topic of the book. Add comments with your signature that includes your website or the name of the book. This is similar to above, but on the regular internet, instead of Facebook itself.

23 | W.C. Madden
Tecumseh's Curse and other titles
www.maddenpublishing.com

I find that doing presentations works somewhat for me. I have spoken to many Rotary clubs about my book, *Tecumseh's Curse*. I'm a Rotarian and find that helps. I also do festivals in the summer to help sell the book and that seems to work. I have a poster of seven presidents crossed out to make people curious about *Tecumseh's Curse* and it works like a charm. I also use some of the social media. I did a video on YouTube, Facebook, Twitter and others. That helps as well. Since most of my books are local in topic, I do a lot of local signings, speeches to groups, talks at libraries and other publicity that's free. Advertising is just too expensive to make it worth my while. Some use eBay and Craigslist to sell their books.

24 | Melinda Iverson Inn
Becoming Your Own Intuitive Healer; The Spirit of Dowsing
www.melindaiversoninn.com

I made all books available as hard copies and eBook copies. I uploaded to Amazon for sale. I wrote to and went to all bookstores in my area (100 mile radius) that might want to carry my book.

I sent a copy to Google Books for uploading. I sent out newsletters to my elist with excerpts of the book as articles with links back to my blog and my website shopping page. Sent above articles to my niche community magazines for publishing with links back to website for purchase.

Gift with purchase: a free eBook of a lesser priced book with a hard copy purchase of one of my other books.

I sent copies to distributors for consideration. I take all my book titles to conferences in my area of expertise to sell.

Bloggers have posted about my books on different sites relating to my area of expertise. I have paid for advertising in the form of an article in magazines in my field.

25 | Paul H. Burton, Creator of the QuietSpacing

QuietSpacing® – Regain Command of Your Day, Get More Done, and Enjoy Life More; Done: Time Management Strategies for Regaining Command of Your Day; The Waterfall Effect: Six Principles for Productive Leadership; Send: A Dozen Ways to Make E-mail Productive ... Again
www.quietspacing.com

Offer books at a discounted rate in conjunction with speaking engagements. I offer all books exceeding the first 100 at a 50% discount from MSRP.

I use Smashwords to produce eBooks and distribute them to numerous channels, as well as Kindle Direct for the Amazon channels. These both give me visibility and delivery mechanisms that take no management time in my day.

My only other advice, which applies generically to any marketing efforts by "small players" like myself, is to know and be an expert in your hyper-niche, then own it by being active in all the "social" ways - blogging, commenting, etc. Related to that is to identify and embrace the folks who are your champions ("Connectors" is what Gladwell called them in *The Tipping Point*). Marketing is about awareness and if there's no budget to work with, then it's a word-of-mouth game. That's where the champions can do you the most good.

26 | Nathan Scot Wells
Am I the Enemy; Memoirs of the Stars
www.nathanscotwells.com

The unfortunate truth when it comes to marketing is it's not as easy to just call a few TV stations and mail a few copies of your books. You have to go outside the box and put forth some cash and allow a professional with contacts do their job. Best thing I have ever done for myself is hire a PR Firm. They make the calls, book the appointments, and do the press releases all for me. It's not a cheap investment, but the reward of the word spreading makes it pay off in the long run.

I also highly encourage everyone to make sure they release an audiobook and an eBook from the start. In the digital world we live in today, it's imperative to do so.

Song Ba To
www.thewritingshop.net

As traditional publishing morphs into digital and on-demand publishing and into eBook publishing, one of the biggest losses will be of the old-school distribution and publicity structures those traditional publishers provided. We are currently in an in-between time where the old structures are fading but nothing revolutionary and large scale has come to take its place. So we have to make do. By this I mean that writers will have to take on publicity tasks that a traditional publisher used to do for them.

First, the book should be available on several platforms, as a regular printed book, as a digital on-demand book (individual copies printed only when ordered) and as an eBook (for the Kindle, the Nook and for other emerging eBook systems). I imagine one day soon an eBook put out on one system will be compatible with all other systems, but this is spotty today.

Second, seek out websites such as Goodreads, which provides a cataloging service that includes self-published works. Get the book listed with them.

Third, start Facebook, LinkedIn and Google+ pages for yourself as an author. You might even make a YouTube video about your book. If the video goes viral, so will your book. (I imagine there are or soon will be more social media pages of this sort to use.)

Fourth, start a blog that talks about you and your work, and that provides some other useful information (for example, on book research, creative writing or on the subject you write about).

Fifth, do your legwork, taking copies to bookstores to see if they will stock it. Many will also help you set up a book signing event at their store. Talk to those who do book reviews for your local paper, radio and TV station.

Finally, search out who will be the interest group for your book. Likely, activists among them will have meetings, reunions and the like. My most recent book is a Vietnam War novel and I am a Vietnam Vet. So I went to veterans' reunions and took stacks of my book to sell there.

I imagine there is much more that can be done. For instance, if you have the resources you can buy advertising in traditional media and from such online outlets as Google. Frankly, I am as interested as any author in what succeeds best in getting a book to likely readers, so I will be watching what Mira does as well as other marketing avenues.

The Quick Guide to Small Business Budgeting; I Have QuickBooks: Now What?; How to Open Your Own In-Home Bookkeeping Service
www.inhomebookkeeping.bizland.com

That's the million dollar question. The way marketing and advertising changes, especially with internet marketing, it is hard to answer that without writing a book. Google's click advertising has about a 95% bogus click rate at an average of $1.25 to $5.00 per click to be on the first page; I quit my AdWords campaign all together. That was the majority of my marketing. I used to be with Baker & Taylor until after tens of thousands of dollars worth of wholesale inventory was purchased I found out that at 89 days they returned about 65% of the inventory damaged and clearly read. If a store orders from me, I accept no returns and pre-payment is required. Otherwise, I won't sell to them. Amazon is the best place for self-published authors. Being on the advantage program and Kindle. It is too costly to compete anywhere else.

29 | John C. Henningson
A Reluctant Warrior 1968-1974; A Vietnam Veteran's Memoir; Adirondack Cabin Stories; Fifty Years in the Wilderness

I make up email lists of family, friends, former classmates from high school and college, neighbors, business associates, etc. I prepare a notice of my publication and send it out to each group which adds up to 200-300 names. Next I ask local bookstores or libraries to advertise a reading/book signing event in the local newspaper. Then I find websites which tend to be associated with the subject matter of my books and ask them to review my book and put the review in their newsletter on the website.

Entertainment Electrics: Electricity for Entertainment Electricians & Technicians; Automated Lighting: The Art and Science of Moving Light; Lighting Design for Modern Houses of Worship and Focus on Lighting Technology
www.APTXL.com

Write for at least one hour each and every day and you'll have a book before you know it. Don't self-edit while you're writing; just let it flow and then come back to it with a fresh perspective and make it better. Don't wait for anyone to approve your idea or book; just do it. Once you have a finished product, learn to use social media to promote it. The media landscape changes often, so stay on top of it and learn to reach as many people as you can with the least amount of effort. Once you've finished your first project, start on the next because you learn something every time and you'll get better and better at it.

Good marketing makes a big difference in book sales. My first book was published by a small publisher in England and they did very little to market it. Consequently the sales were not spectacular. My second book was published by a big publishing company, and their approach was 180 degrees from the first publisher, which made a huge difference in sales.

First, they asked me for an outline and the first chapter, and they sent it to about two or three dozen different college professors (this book was targeted for the education market) to get feedback about the proposed book. I incorporated the feedback into the book and those professors who replied felt like they had a stake in the book, so a lot of them now use it for their courses.

Secondly, the big publishing company attends a lot of trade shows and markets the book directly. That helps sales quite a bit. Again, this book is very specific to a particular market, so it's easy to find those trade shows.

Thirdly, once you have a book published, speaking opportunities open up. Take advantage of them because they help raise your profile and help sell books. And you don't need a publisher to do these things. If your book is more mainstream, these things won't help.

Whether it's a mainstream book or a targeted book, the game is rapidly changing and there are a lot of social media outlets to promote book sales. There are almost a billion people on Facebook, and it's not hard to build a following if you put some time into growing your list of friends. There's also Twitter, Instagram, Tumblr, ad nauseam. These all present a wealth of opportunities to connect with potential readers. I consistently tweet and post on Facebook but I'm careful not to post trivia. Every time I post I try to post something compelling, useful, funny, or informative. Then your followers grow to a sizable number, which gives you the opportunity to reach a lot of people very quickly and easily.

When I have an event like a workshop, seminar, or speaking event, I tweet it and post it on Facebook. When people reply, I always make sure to acknowledge it so they feel like they're connected to you. It helps build a connection and helps them buy into your brand. As an author, you have to take charge of your own marketing, take advantage of the internet, and actively promote your product if you want sales to grow.

31 | Sue (Cooley) Blesi
Where Dead Men Still Fight: A History of Stanton, Missouri; Gleanings From the Past: Volume I: 1991-1996; Union
www.missourikidpress.com

First, find a distributor. They get about 55 percent, but they'll get books into the big bookstores for you. Sounds like a lot, but that's the cost of doing business. (Just remember, you saved on your printing by going to MIRA.) The bookstores get 40 percent and the big ones often won't deal with an author directly. We used a distributor for Dan's ghost books and it worked fine. We use Partners Book Distributors, Inc. (Sam Speigel sspeigel@partners-east.com, 517-694-3205). At the time we contracted with them, there were four distributors dealing with small presses that Barnes and Noble was willing to deal with. Unfortunately, there are none in St. Louis anymore that I am aware of. ?

Make up a professional marketing package for your distributor with a photo of the book cover and information about the book, and a little information about the author as well. Store a professional color flyer on your computer to send to anyone interested.

To do your own marketing, contact bookstores and LIBRARIES in your target area, introduce yourself (email is fine), make a sales pitch and include the flyer. Sometimes other local businesses will be willing to carry your book(s) as well, but you will have to walk in and discuss it with them. Offer to do a book signing at any bookstores, libraries, or other businesses you are willing to drive (fly) to. Making up nice color bookmarks and/or flyers to pass out or for the store/library to hand out in advance is a nice touch. You can get library email addresses by searching for libraries in each state. Don't send to a lot of libraries at one time or your emails will end up in their junk email or labeled as spam. Bookstores will want 40 percent.

Another way to market is through a magazine that caters to your target market. If you are selling a cookbook, a cooking magazine would be good. If, as in Dan's case, your books are on the paranormal, find a paranormal magazine. This is expensive, but if you think you can sell them this way, go for it.

Another way to sell is through the media. Dan has been on the radio, television, and featured in newspapers. He talks about the paranormal and they plug his book. The more of this you can do, the better, because it doesn't cost you anything.

Another way is to contact whoever does book reviews for newspapers and magazines. You will have to give them a free copy and they might have a lot ahead of you. If your book is national in scope, you can do this with newspapers throughout the country. It takes time. Be sure to let your distributor and major bookstores know when such a release is coming out in a specific area so they can have books on hand to meet the demand.

And, get it on Amazon.com. Find someone who has a full-fledged Amazon.com bookstore and ask them to list the book for you, providing them with a .jpg of the cover, and a short description, including a list of search words. In Dan's case, that list would include ghosts, paranormal, haunted, and probably 20 other words that would trigger the title in Amazon's search engine. If you can't find someone to do this for you, sooner or later, someone will eventually list your book; then you can sign up to sell your book through Amazon without having to pay the $40/month fee the bigger booksellers pay. If you don't pay that fee, you are not allowed to create new listings. Then, get all your friends to "review" your book on Amazon.com.

Be slow to do consignments. After having half a dozen small shops close their doors and not return my books, I only have two businesses I am still willing to do consignment with but do sell small quantities to stores that I don't mind driving to when they run out.

For my local histories, I don't need a distributor. I just sell to local bookstores, historical societies, and individuals. Selling to individuals cuts out the middle man and you put more in your pocket for each book sold. It is important to keep your retail price the same for all venues or you will have some unhappy customers.

If you're already talking to MIRA, you have probably already figured this out, but be leery of big publishing companies that offer to print your book and sell it for you. I understand many of them have it in their contract that they do not take returns. Some small ones might do this as well. Distributors (which is the way to get your book into the big bookstores) will not do business with them because they have to be able to take returns when the store is unable to sell the books. In addition, these places price books too high, which makes it harder to sell them. Often, they don't edit at all, or maybe only run spell check on it.

I have no connection to MIRA or to Partners Book Distributors, Inc., but have been using MIRA for all of my printing. I have also sent self-publishing authors, whose works I have edited and set up in InDesign, to MIRA and they have all been happy with their books.

Before you print, find a good editor. Even if you taught English for 30 years, chances are good that you are not as good an editor as you think; plus you are less likely to see the errors you made! If you didn't teach English for 30 years, don't even think about it. I have a stack of books that were proofread by the author or by a friend who taught English, and I can show you mistakes in all of them. Books that are full of errors or not set up professionally turn readers off, hurt your sales, and are less likely to hold the attention of big publishers who might want to turn your small press book into a national bestseller. I am an editor and I <u>always</u> have someone else read my books and my weekly newspaper columns before they are published. In addition, an editor who works in the field should be able to point out some of the pitfalls he/she sees in your book that might get you into legal trouble. Self-publishing is a wonderful opportunity for you to get your books on the market, but there are a lot of books out there now that reflect poorly on the author due to no editing or bad editing. Do it right!

32 | **Vincent Ferguson**
Six Weeks to a Six Pack; Get Ready, Get Set, Get Fit
www.sixweeks.com

Besides the traditional ways like Amazon, Barnes & Noble, etc., I sell most of my books at events, workshops and speaking engagements. Since my book is about fitness and I'm always sponsoring or conducting fitness-related events, my books sell quickly. I carved out a niche market and built a strong reputation on being an expert in the field of fitness, so it's been relatively easy to sell my books.

I've also found it helpful to link up with a charity and offer a portion of the proceeds from my book to go towards that charity.

It also doesn't hurt to give your book its own web address and website. I even created a fitness contest that cost $10.00 to enter and in exchange for entering the contest you received a free copy of my fitness eBook. Needless to say I received lots of publicity and money, all from a contest on my eBook website.

I am quite well-known in Norway as I have been teaching and coaching for over 30 years. That means that I have a big "hot network." I think that is where one has to start.

Inform your family and friends and all who know you in any place you have been. The ones who know you are the best contacts for marketing.

Then you need to connect your work/book with your name and picture. I have used my picture as the favicon on the Norwegian homepage and the English blog page.

I invited two well-known people from different groups to write forewords in my book. And I thanked many people in my foreword, so when someone sees the name, they make the connection.

I already had a homepage for my school and a personal homepage, both with blogs. I have used these, of course.
I have given out 200 books to important networking people and to journalists who have written about me. I launched my book at a big alternative fair/meeting (Europe's biggest in Oslo, Norway).

I give lectures for groups and schools and involve myself in discussions on Facebook. I use Facebook and have several pages in Norwegian and English.

Above and Beyond Wellfleet: A Memoir about
Welcoming Life after Loss
www.tinytomespublishing.com

It's wild and wooly out there in the world of publishing, but I have found so far that self-publishing at the moment beats being at the mercy of a publisher who owns your hard work. It seems that the days of large advances—particularly for new, untested authors—are over.

I am fortunate in several ways. This is not my day job, although it is a job I take very seriously. I did get an offer to have my book listed through Vantage Press (a very respectable house catering to self-publishing). The rub was the contract called for a large (to me) outlay of money for their services AND they would have owned my book for two years. I turned down the offer, but was encouraged by their review of the book.

My over 30 years professional experience was in Communications and Public Relations so while I have hired experts to help me along the way, I am a pretty good judge of what I need and what I don't.

Having said that--here are a few tips.

Before you print the book, seek the advice of a good editor and graphic designer. No matter how simple the book or how good a writer you are, it is imperative that the book be well edited and proofed. Have lots of people proof the book before it gets printed.

The book is the best marketing tool in the beginning. Swallow your pride and ask bookstores, galleries and libraries to carry it. Give it away to as many people as you can who you think can help build your reputation.

Find one bookstore that will be willing to sell the book online--Amazon is the logical choice.

Yoking Up with Jesus and Kingdom of God
Government; Understanding the Working of Faith;
How to Obtain Financial Freedom Workbook
www.amazon.com

Please see my lists of some things that have worked for me.

1. I try to keep up with the events that are with various states. This can be done by contacting the convention center; they have a schedule of all the events for the year. I contact these sponsors to see if I can be a vendor, and they reply with table information (size and cost).

2. I check with the library and they usually have various newspapers with local events listed.

3. I have traveled the East coast visiting various Army bases to set up as a vendor and this has worked very well.

4. I am invited to different churches as a guest speaker. I have done very well.

5. From time to time I have listed my books in some of the most popular newspapers.

6. I have done commercial ads for TV.

7. I am in the process of placing my books on Amazon.com and Barnes and Noble.

8. I have set up book signings at some of the local bookstores.

9. I have done some email marketing.

10. My number one marketing strategy is word of mouth—talking to the people with whom I do business, or those I meet at the gas station, grocery store, bank, etc.

*Cinnamon: A season of poems; Little Buddy
Udsy; Malik's Giggling Snowman; Teeth For
Thanksgiving; Roger, You're A Mess; Uncle J.J.'s
Band; Hurricane T.*

I would suggest joining one of the book publishing organizations like SPAN, IBPA, or another. They are not just for companies; they do accept writers, or any other interested party. There is a membership fee. But they do keep you up on what's happening in the publishing industry, who's accepting what, who to avoid sending your work to, and they offer lots of other advice. The good thing about it is you can call them for advice or other information, and if they don't have it at the time, they'll research it for you. (Make them work for the fee.) They also keep you informed on book fairs, and how to get your books on display.

Second, I would try to find an agent—one who has been around for a while, and one who has established a good reputation. Again, the publishing organizations can be of help here. Don't be afraid to try wholesalers or distributors. Some will not represent single title authors, but there are a few that will.

37 | William A. Patrick III
Khing; Linder in Brazil; Dealer's Dog
www.amazon.com

Originally I had it listed by a self-publishing company that, like most companies out there catering to unknown writers, just took my money.

But one way to get your stuff out there is to join or use different groups or sites on the web, like writers groups, or even Kindle groups. I submitted a postcard to postsecret.com mentioning that I had a book that nobody would read. It got readers because it was mentioned to the site's large audience.

I turned *KHING* into a kindle download, and I use the printed copies, listing them myself as "if you have one to sell" to get it out there. It has about 200 likes and is the most success I've had yet. Even then I only sold about 50 books, and those at a net loss because of discounts, shipping and printing costs. But at least it's out there, somewhere.

Also, *Linder in Brazil* is carried in The Birdwatcher, a store in Julian, CA, because it has a bird list inside and because we know the owners. They use the proceeds to spay stray cats.

My biggest marketing tool right now is word of mouth. However, I have success with the following, as well:

1) Facebook ads
2) Promotional calendars, pens, etc. passed out at speaking engagements
3) Website promotions (i.e. contests)

39 | Rosemary Pollock
A Friend to All: The Life and Contributions of Dr. John Fuller Weld (1808-1892)

Since my book is based on primary research or personal eighteenth-century letters, I have been sending complimentary copies to all of the people who have assisted me in the process. For instance, the Harvard Countway Medical Library, the Nauvoo Historical Society, the Minnesota Historical Society (where the letters originated), and any other key person I talked to or contacted while gathering my research. Hopefully this will allow me to have some recognition among these key resource centers as well as exposure to academic institutions.

I am also going to prepare a flyer with a copy of the cover on the flyer to send to key universities that I know would be interested in the material. I am also going to be speaking about the book at two events and have book signings at this time.

Living the Low Sodium Life: A Practical Guide and Recipes

Given that my book is for people who have heart or kidney problems, I sent complimentary copies to cardiologists and nephrologists along with posters detailing information about how to order. I also targeted local pharmacies and the local library and presented my book to the area Coalition for Women with heart disease.

41 | Yolanda Brunson-Sarrabo

Another Face of Multiple Myeloma; The ins and outs of the fashion industry from a fashion insider
www.madaboutmyeloma.com
www.ybrunson.com

Publishing your own work is not an easy feat; however, there are different avenues to consider in getting the most out of selling your book.

5 Musts

1. Establish a website- This is an imperative tool to sell your book directly and a great way to market the product.

2. Gear up for social media- In these changing times, it is very important to be familiar with the various social media networks available: Twitter, Facebook, Instagram, Pinterest, and LinkedIn.

3. Associated networks- If your book is about health, you should do research on the magazines that would appreciate what you have to say on a specific topic and then make reference that you're an author and have written about this particular topic. As a self-published author you will have to work a bit harder in getting into these publications, but it's possible, and it opens up another audience for you.

4. Press Release- Promote yourself with a press kit that details your book, ISBN, retail cost, contact information, and bio. This package can be sent directly to publications to achieve possible write-ups in their publication and alert the audience about the author- which depends if the audience

of that publication has a need to hear about your story. Promote with free press releases at try-biblioscribe.com.

5. Seek interviews- Reach out to local newspapers and/or smaller web radio forums, use your press release kit and investigate if there would be an interest in your book and interviewing you about the book.

A Journey with Poppies; The Head of Khalid Salaam; Frigby's War
www.amazon.com
www.authorhouse.com

One of the most pressing issues that comes up at our Writers' Guild is how to sell our wares. I presume you are referring to self-published authors when you ask the question and I'll base my answer on that assumption. Of course, traditionally published authors are not immune from being involved in the promotion process either. It's just that they usually have help from the publisher. The self-published author is on his/her own for the most part.

Here are some things I have learned over the years and our writer's group is learning what works and what doesn't. I'm not sure the following constitute the Holy Grail of book promotion, but they are better than sitting home waiting for book buyers to hunt you down and demand to purchase your work.

1. The first rule is that the work (novel, biography, cookbook, whatever) must actually be a piece of literature, relatively easy to read, interesting, and written for the reader. If the product is garbage, then all the promotion in the world won't sell it. In addition, it must have appeal. There is a fellow in our guild who wrote an 800 page book on a little-known WWII aircraft. The book is not garbage, but it's interesting to one person in a million. So, along with the above criteria, it must appeal to wide audience.

2. The author must devote time and effort to the promotion process. He/she must overcome reluctance to promote his/her work. It's the hardest thing for many to do. Authors prefer to write, not promote. I know; I'm one.

3. Expanding on #1 above, it is best if the product appeals to many segments of the reading population. If the potential readers come from a narrow segment, finding them will be more difficult. Not impossible, but harder. The vast majority of the reading public are women. Books that don't interest women will mostly be bought by women as a gift for a man who will not get around to reading it. Lesson here is--write a book that will appeal to both genders. There are exceptions, as in the case of Tom Clancyesque action novels. Still, women rule.

4. Join a local writer's group. There is benefit in seeing what others do and have done; plus presentations by groups will be accepted by organizations, libraries, etc., whereas a single individual's might not.

5. Develop a spiel--a good one. Actually, develop several spiels. You need one when you address the local Rotary Club. You need one tailored to a local book club. You need one when sitting at a table at the local art fair and you are dealing one-on-one with a prospective buyer. In short, your presentation needs to be professional, polished, brief, and target the audience.

6. These spiels are focused mostly on why your book will be of interest to the person(s) you are speaking

with. However, a few words about you and why you wrote the book are appropriate, as well as what gives you the credibility to write on the subject. All of this should be done with the utmost humility, as braggarts rarely sell books.

7. Use the media. If you can get written up in a newspaper or magazine, great. Make contact with radio and TV stations. Tell them you would be available to be on the air anytime they have a spot open. Normally it is best to do this in person or by phone. Make contact with an actual person. Afterward, send them a confirmation letter, thanking them in advance for any opportunity that they provide and include a synopsis of your book and a short biography of yourself. If you haven't heard anything in six weeks, call and ask to speak to the person you made contact with in the first place. Be prepared for rejection.

8. You need a website or several websites. If your publisher provides a site, put that on a business card. One card for each book/site. It won't hurt for you to have your own site pointing the buyer to the publisher site for more info/purchase.

9. You will need a war chest of stuff if you go to book signings. Bookmarks with your name, book, website, etc. are great give-aways. A bowl of edible goodies can be valuable. We have one guy who makes cookies for his table. Include a drape for the table, a display rack, name plate, business cards, posters on easels advertising your book, and chairs for the visitors.

10. **Publicity is key in anything you do.** If you are going to speak at the local business person's luncheon, call everyone you know in the organization or who might be inclined to visit just to hear you. If you are scheduled for a book signing, notify the local newspapers and other media, call friends and ask them to tell their friends. If you simply go to the book signing, spread your war chest on the table and wait for the throng to appear, you will be disappointed. Sometimes, even with publicity, that happens. Unfortunately, in this day and age, people have too many distractions competing for their time. Buying and reading your book is usually low on their priority list. They need enticement.

11. **Identify your target audience** and focus your efforts on them. If you've written a book on pottery making, your audience will come from craft shops, craft fairs, etc. and your media will be the magazines and radio shows that deal with crafts. I wrote a book about experiences in Vietnam. I found that ninety percent of my sales came from veterans. I contacted numerous military organizations, local veterans groups, etc. In fact, if you go to the O'Fallon VFW you will find a bookshelf of local authors' work containing a couple of my books. Our guild got that going and, although it's just underway, the manager tells us he's had numerous inquiries about some of the material displayed. The jury is still out on how successful that will be.

Okay, so much for the stuff we have learned, mostly through the school of hard knocks. The greatest challenge for the self-published author is not the drafting, not the editing, not the publishing--it is the promotion. There is a niche market out there that some self-publishing houses are trying to tap, but I believe they are misguided. They offer fantastic media blitz activities, full-page advertisements in the New York Times, thousands of hand-outs mailed to newspapers, etc. Of course, this comes at a price most self-published authors can't afford. The publisher is not invested in the success of the venture in any way. They don't really care if the book sells or not because they have their money.

43 | Chris Simpkin
Editor of *Bigfoot Blues;* author of *The Log Cabin Gas Station* (published by Chris-Chris, LLC) *and G-Eye* (published by High Hill Press)
www.haldsimpkin.com

I would suggest all your authors belong to at least one writers group. There are several in the St. Louis Metropolitan area. My first choice is the St. Louis Writers Guild. Founded in 1920, it is one of the oldest and largest literary organizations in the Midwest. Members receive access to their webinars, free workshops, access to critique groups and promotion of books. Other groups I can recommend are The Missouri Chapter of Sisters in Crime, Saturday Writers, and the St. Louis Publishers Association. Dues for all these groups are very reasonable. Check their websites for specific services offered. Recommend that your authors have someone edit their book before it is printed. Any of the organizations listed above can recommend editors.

For book promotion, we worked with Dianna Graveman, owner of 2 Rivers Communications & Design, LLC. She helped promote Hal's books online. Among other services, she'll establish a website or blog and connect the author to sites like Goodreads. Her website is www.2rivers communications.com. She's very easy to work with and worth the money.

There is a free website, www.WritingForDollars.com that contains many tips about writing and marketing. There probably are others but this is the one I read.

Other than that, each author must be as creative as possible. Think about the audience for your book. Contact those groups. Make friends with independent bookstore owners. Consider a book signing. (Sometimes those sell books.)

Marketing is the hardest part of being an author but interacting with other authors saves time. They'll tell you what worked for them.

PharmDceutics: Applied Biopharmaceutics for Clinical Pharmacists
www.pharmdceutics.com

We have been marketing the book three ways.

1. We set up a website to sell it, using PayPal to accept credit cards. After much looking, for a small business this seemed like the best low-cost solution.

2. Since it's a college textbook, we have sent information and offered free review copies to professors who might use it in their courses. This information is found by looking at the pharmacy school websites and using the directories. We have contacted about half of the pharmacy schools so far and will continue to contact the remainder shortly after the first of the year. Since students don't buy textbooks they aren't required to have, the professor is the real "market maker." It's a bit of work to change textbooks for a course, so this may take a little while to generate sales. But free review copies is really the only way to get a professor to seriously consider a book.

3. We submitted it to three different venues for professional reviews. One is a listserv for pharmacists who might be interested. The other two are academic journals that include textbook reviews. A positive review by either of these academic journals is probably the best thing.

45 | George Anne Brown
El Loro Es Verde; The Ponce de Leon of Boca Raton
www.donscheer.com

Bookster.com is a platform for authors to connect with and grow their fan base. Most importantly, it will be a platform for authors to make incremental revenue from their fans by selling signed books, phone consultations, video conference consultations, meet and greets, exclusive/bonus/pre-release content, and many other creative ways to engage fans and sell them additional things besides just books. Authors will hand out some really creative "rewards" when they do a Kickstarter publishing project, like "I will include your name as a character in my book for $1,000," or "I will meet you and 3 friends for coffee to discuss writing tips or just chat for $2,000." The only limit is the author's creativity, because we provide loads of defaults but the author gets to choose what he or she offers and how much he or she will charge.

46 | Valerie J. Lewis Coleman
The Forbidden Secrets of the Goody Box; Self-Publishing Made Easy Journals; Blended Families: An Anthology; Tainted Mirror: An Anthology; Lord, Help Me to Hold Out
www.PenOfTheWriter.com
www.TheGoodyBoxBook.com

Most authors are right-brained introverts. The thought of having to engage with readers can be frightening and overwhelming. Having attended hundreds of book fairs, I witnessed authors sitting behind tables, watching potential customers walk past. In my experience, incorporating the following ideas can help improve your book sales:

Pre-event
Individual promotion is essential to ensure that people come to the event specifically for you. Emails, texts, phone calls and social media are great tools to invite people. Post the event on your website, Facebook and your Amazon author page. Invite book clubs and writers' groups. These audiences are avid readers who often look for book fairs, authors and writing resources. Posting your participation to online community calendars and sites that blast media releases is helpful. Contacting local media for possible interviews or articles can attract new fans.

Event
Table presentation. If your display appeals to the eyes, readers will be more inclined to stop for a chat. Consider bright colors, staging in tiers and candy. Offering a freebie (book, promotional item, etc.) is a great way to attract visitors and collect emails.

Engage the book lovers. The table can be a place of comfort for the shy author and it can also be a barrier to connecting with your readers. Consider the vendor carts at malls. Are you more likely to peruse the product of the sales person who stands, greets you and then invites you to "check out the merchandise" or the one who sits on the stool with his back to you? Take on the persona of the sales person who works on commission: energetic, friendly and attentive! If they like you, they will be more inclined to buy from you.

Speak. If the opportunity is available, speak about your book. I sell more books when I deliver an entertaining and engaging presentation. The technique has landed subsequent speaking engagements and significant book sells.

Nonverbal communication is more powerful than spoken words (the experts say that only 7% of a message is conveyed with words). Body posture, stance, handshakes, smiles, eye contact, tone, volume, pitch and more affect the message. Remember, actions speak louder than words.

WIIFM. What's in it for me? The reader has to see value in your book. Ask a couple of questions to find out what's important to them and then make sure your sales pitch meets that need. Keep it short and sweet. For example, I pitch my novel, *The Forbidden Secrets of the Goody Box*, several ways: For women, my spiel includes that I surveyed men and listened while they had that barber-shop, locker-room, man-cave conversation to which women aren't normally privy to divulge relationship secrets that help women better understand men. For fathers of daughters, I explain that a father is the first protector of the goody box and if he wants his daughter(s) to avoid the heartache and pitfalls of bad relationship decisions, this book helps start that sometimes difficult conversation about dating and sex. For pastors and youth leaders, I focus on the fact that the book is a call to abstinence that complements the teachings of the Bible.

Accept credit cards. Paypal.com offers a mobile card reader that works on smart phones to accept credit cards. The program features are simple: free device, no contract and a 2.7% transaction fee. Visit paypal.com for more details.

Post-event
Follow-up is important. Send a thank you email to the organizer and your new fans.

Here are a couple of shorter ideas:

I created eight-page booklets using Publisher (two 8.5" x 11" sheets printed double-sided). The booklets include the book cover and synopsis, copyright page, reviews, first chapter, bio and order form with contact and purchasing info. I give them away at trade shows, drive-through windows and anywhere I meet potential customers. The booklets prove to be most effective when I conduct workshops or present on the topic of the book.

Include information and links to purchase your books at the bottom of every email you send. Most email providers have a feature that allows you to compose an automatic signature.

Military bases are great venues. Consider signing at the high-traffic areas where military and non-military personnel work: hospital, headquarters, etc.

47 | Dr. Luis A. Rosado
Desarrollo del Español; Los Pasteles de Coco
www. allbilingualteachers.com

Write a book with your audience in mind. Identify a need and possible consumers. If the expected earnings justify the effort, write the book.

Be sure you secure ISBNs and that your book is copyrighted appropriately. It means you will have to pay a fee and send a copy of the publication to the Library of the Congress.

Do not list a price on the cover of the book. This will discourage distributors, who might buy your book in bulk to sell them to a third party.

Make updates to the product to be sure that you are keeping up with changes.

Write academic articles and mention your book.

Make presentations at state and national conferences, even if no honorarium is allocated, where you indirectly mention your publications. If you present just to introduce your book, most people will see it as a "sales pitch."

If you are writing short stories for children, do not create spaces so that students can answer comprehension questions in the book. This will make it a workbook, and libraries do not want to encourage children to write on books.

Invite your friends to a formal *book presentation*. Ask one of your friends to host it for you, even if you pay for the event.

Identify associations or civic groups that might be interested in buying your product, and offer to buy breakfast or lunch if they allow you to present your product.

If you are a college instructor, design a class where your book can become the textbook. Be sure to request approval from your institution prior to assigning it as the textbook for the course.

A Cultural Legacy: CREOLE Gourmet Secrets of Louisiana; Louisiana's French Creole Culinary & Linguitic Traditions: Facts vs. Fiction Before and Since Cajunization; Speaking in Tongues: Louisiana's French Colonial, Afro-Creole & Cajun Languages Speak For Themselves
www.creolebookstore.com

Use questions to get people thinking and post them on Facebook or in newspaper ads or in starting conversations. And, never consign books after you've published and sold successfully. You lose inventory, risk damage to books and you lose money. Direct sales or wholesaling guarantees maximum profits for re-investment, distribution of dividends to co-authors or photographers, etc.

Your book should be beautiful in appearance, which will enhance its perceived value, and people are more inclined to tell others about it and show it off, as well as to buy it for gifting.

Finding your "niche" or area of expertise is critical to your success because you must know what you're talking about and you must target that audience who shares this area of interest. Hopefully, it is one which attracts and appeals to a wide audience such as ethnic groups, historians, libraries, academia, college bookstores, businesses and most especially, everyday people who value learning for themselves and their children.

1) Spread the word to friends & family
2) Internet/website and press releases
3) Friends of the Library groups
4) Public, State & private libraries
5) Guest lectures/book sales at civic club groups
6) Vendor table at festivals, flea markets
7) Facebook announcements and updates
8) Direct sales/private, independent bookstores
9) "Bookshops" at conventions (ex. Rotary Club)
10) Foreign Language/Cultural Forums/chat rooms via internet
11) Local television & radio interviews
12) Gifting friends or individuals who are affiliated with special interests/charitable associations groups with free copies to spread interest
13) Conversation starters with people who show interest anywhere/everywhere
14) Consignments/wholesaling to restaurant, café and book/gift shops
15) Hospital gift shops
16) Chambers of Commerce/Museum bookstores/shops
17) Digital books via Amazon.com, Bookrix.com etc.
18) Hire student sales reps. for commission on every book sold
19) At my guesthouse B&B/Food Club membership includes discounts on Guesthouse bookstore purchases
20) Networking with co-authors to foster sales in their localities
21) Book promotion services over internet
22) Ingram or any other independent book distributors who won't devour your profit + production costs

23) Newspaper ads in many states/major cities
24) Book Club/Cultural magazine ads/interviews in lieu of payment for ads
25) Direct Sales marketing travel to other cities, states doing advanced homework locating/communicating with bookstore, gift shop, cafe/restaurant, cooking schools
26) Volunteer cooking for group/individual fundraisers/charitable causes with sell book option
27) Donation of portion of proceeds for charitable causes/organizations/schools/church fundraisers, etc.
28) Book distributors who are willing to negotiate terms/commissions so author isn't swindled, or at least receives a decent portion of money from sales
29) Walmart if book is for general public interests (only my cookbooks are appropriate here)
30) Reserve books for give-aways to individuals or educators who you know would influence or network with other people who share interests in your book's subject matter
31) Garage & Rummage, Treasure & Trash Summer/Fall Sales at home

Independent bookstores on Manhattan's West Side refused to consider a self-published poetry book for consignment. I managed to get a few copies on the shelves of the Jewish Museum, the JCC Manhattan and West Side Judaica bookstores. Sales were spotty.

Our first book reading and party for relatives and friends, on a nasty Sunday afternoon, at my son's apartment in Washington Heights, was a success. Many books purchased were intended as gifts for friends and clients. A book reading was held after hours at a local food store that had tables. Circulars were posted in the lobbies of neighborhood multiple dwellings. The event was jointly sponsored by a health tea company. The video made by my daughter-in-law included readings by a public speaking instructor and an actress, and is available at www.youtube.com.

Extracts were beautifully read at the poetry club of the Ethical Culture Society, by my neighbor who was a member. All ages are welcomed by Poetry Place. Recently on a Sunday afternoon of poetry readings, I read *My Father, He Knew About Love* by the benches on the Riverside Drive Island at 103rd Street.

Seven poems from *Thoughts of Being* which have Jewish themes, such as *Daniel (For Daniel Pearl)* and *Yizkor: A Train to Auschwitz* were printed in *The Queens College Journal of Jewish Studies, Volume XIV*. The Editor-in-Chief, after purchasing a copy and deeming the poems appropriate, obtained permission to include them provided that attribution was given. Direct sales marketing was done at the Farmers Market, West 97th Street, between Columbus and Amsterdam Avenues, Friday mornings, and at the Central Park Tennis House, and on the paths to and from. The people I approach are often reading or inactive. With an open book in hand, I ask, "May I show you my brother's poetry book?"

I have prepared a tri-part folded paper handout, 6 in. x 3 in. On one face is a pictorial of the cover. The other 2/3 synopses the author and book, provides the ISBN, cost, and where purchasable. The handout is offered where purchase hesitancy is expressed. It is also made available where Nook, Kindle, iPad or iPhone-type usage is feasible.

A table to display copies of the book can often be found at musical and community events tenants and membership meetings.

*Loving Life...all of it: A Walk with Cancer, Compassion
and Consciousness*
www.amycamie.com

1. Share your manuscript with several people who understand and work within the topic of your book before publishing, and ask for testimonials from credible sources. For my book, I asked leaders in the cancer field, prominent physicians, therapists and social workers to offer testimonials that I could use on my back cover, website and for promotional purposes.

2. Create a special event around the theme of your new book and use the event as a book release. I am a harpist whose book is about my journey with breast cancer so I scheduled a concert in my hometown and asked one of the cancer centers to help sponsor the event.

3. For digital conversion and eBook distribution, I chose Bookbaby.com. They have a couple different pricing options, will convert your file for all readers and then send your book out their partner sites which include: Apple's iBookstore, Amazon, Barnes & Noble, Sony Reader Store, Kobo, and more. You're in control from start to finish and retain all publishing and ownership rights. They're a one stop shop!

Take the time to edit your book, and when you are finished find a very good proofreader and copy editor to do it again. Make your book available to the press prior to releasing with courtesy copies.

The Tin Man: The Voice of an Incest Survivor; Hand in Hand: A True Life Story
www.tinmanministries.com

I have been very successful in selling my books when I do a speaking engagement. I usually sell most of my books when I do. I also have a workshop that I created in which my book *The Tin Man* is a required read. I run these workshops several times throughout the year. On the final day of the workshop, I offer my book *Hand in Hand* to be sold.

53 | Pricilla (PJ) Cowan

Giggle-Grump-Gurgle; Michael O'Brien and the Magic Hat; Tilbee Toadlet's Trip to Town
www.storiesbypj.com

The best marketing tool in my opinion is to schedule book signings at grocery stores and book shops. Buy a table at a flea market or craft fair. Folks are more likely to buy if they meet you face to face.

You need good content and you need a great cover that has the color red in it. If there is red in the cover, it increases sales by 50%. The cover must inspire the buying public to pick it up!

55 | Marilena Minucci, MS, CHC, BCC
*Quantum Coaching Questions: A NOT So Little Book of
BIG Questions for Wellness Coaches; Anyone
Mastering the Art of Asking*
www.QuantumCoachingMethod.com

Creating Buzz and Deepening the Relationship with my potential buyers:

I held a virtual book launch and recorded the call.

I continue to send and post the call recording which speaks heavily about the book content and offers additional incentives including a chance to win a seat at my upcoming training (no purchase necessary).

Finally, I created a six-month virtual book club for anyone who does buy the book so they can really engage in the content. I simply asked everyone who has been so thankful for these calls to pay it forward by recommending the book every month to one other coach they know.

Create and publicize local events for the book. Include non-traditional book signings, book fairs, etc. Try to find events (or create them) that would draw people interested in the topic of your book. This will break your book out of the "friends and family" buyers. My first book signing was at a bookstore, and I brought a chicken! And I also was part of an "urban chicken-raising" seminar at a local nursery.

57 | Nicole Bruno
So What If I Bleed; Fried Fish and Breast Milk; coming soon— Delirium of the Deflowered
www.nicoleborello.com

The internet has been the best tool for marketing for me. Creating a Facebook page and a website to attract more readers has definitely helped in marketing my books. You connect with other poets and publishers and you can promote each other. Both blogs and Facebook let the reader know about any upcoming events, readings, upcoming books and you can post your individual poems as well—a sneak preview, as one might say. These social media sites also give the reader a chance to get to know the poet in a more personal way. I have one of my books on Amazon, which is a great place to have your book just for the exposure alone. Many people are very familiar with and already have accounts set up with Amazon so it is easy for them to just go there and purchase a book.

I started off by self-publishing my first book and then started building my resume. I entered my first book, *So What If I Bleed*, into the International Book Awards and also USA "Best Books" Awards and I was a finalist in both contests. This gave me more exposure as they put me on their website as well, and I was able to get free award images for my website and print material. I submitted individual poems to online magazines and my poems were accepted. This is great exposure too, because they put your bio and website on their website, so readers can go directly to your website from there.

I attended creative writing classes at the local college and after my first book came out, I asked the teacher if I could come and read for the students on the first night of class and she agreed. I now go every semester. This is a great way to get exposure because you get to introduce new students to your work every semester, and make sales right on the spot. You could also suggest to the teacher to recommend the book at the beginning of the semester as an option for course materials.

Things I've done on the side for fun to promote my book: YouTube readings are a great way to expose your work, and they are great because people hear your voice and emotions when you are reading the poem. I just recorded my voice and put the words on the screen with a black background. Some people get fancy and actually make videos of their poems, which is fine, but I just like to stick to the words and emotions of the poem without any distractions. I also have a t-shirt/product line called Nicole's Poetry Shop, where I have taken lines from my poetry or quotes about poetry, and promoting poetry in general and have put them on products. You can have fun with marketing. Once you get your foot in the door, things just keep coasting along.

I have a variety of ideas on how I sell my book, but really my books are designed to sell me. As a professional speaker they give me credibility with potential clients. I love to send them free books, and then get hired for a nice fee to speak. My book is a great marketing piece. The average person still has a sense of great reverence for books.

But the way to sell the books is by being a speaker/expert at conferences. Then I offer them at the back of the room after my speaking engagement.

I have 3 books now, so I offer them as a package: buy 2 and get the 3rd free. People love that. I spoke recently to about 50 people and sold $500 dollars worth of books. The advantage is that people don't throw away books. They are a permanent business card. If they have heard you speak and they are someday involved in hiring speakers for an association, then you may be called for a speaking engagement. It has worked for me many, many times.

Certainly, list them on Amazon.com—that is easy—and let people know they can buy them there. Be sure to order the ISBN for your books so you can list them on Amazon.com.

It's hard work.

1. Store on Amazon, or work with a publisher on Amazon. We work with Aegis Journal - easy people to work with.
2. We submitted the book to many reviewers - both pre- and post-publication.
3. We work with associations to sell the book.
4. We blogged about the books.
5. The authors spoke at conventions and the books were offered for sale.
6. As these were professional books, many were discussed in professional forums by friends and/or champions of the author...

Alaska Titan in the Cruise Ship Theme Park; Cannabis North Non-Fiction: Make a Thousand; Gear List of the Golden Moon

The single best piece of advice I got in physically publishing a book was "A lot of good books go down because of bad layout." The woman who told me that knows what she's talking about. I've hired a layout artist for all four of my books. Same person on the last three. I give him a clear idea of what I want, he either takes that and makes it better or he says, "We can do it but I think you'll be disappointed if we use this." That's why I pay him. He's the artist and he's got good instincts. If it's something I feel strongly the book needs we talk about why it's important and he figures out how to incorporate that. Get someone recommended by another author, preferably get someone in town because they know word of mouth makes or breaks their business.

The layout artist isn't someone you want to edit your book. A) They charge by the hour and they charge a lot. B) The good ones are busy and can't/don't want to spend a lot of time looking through your book for mistakes. There will always be some amendments you'll want to make, a misspelling or missing word perhaps, when you see the proof but substantial rewrites will be expensive for you and irritating for the layout artist.

Well-known authors with multiple printings will sometimes admit to being appalled by the layout a large publishing house has created for one of their books. One of the cool things about publishing your own book is that you have the final say in how it looks.

A lot of conventional wisdom I got (and still get from people) on publishing isn't current. So many authors do eBooks thinking they can do something like colors on the computer but couldn't do the same thing on paper, when the case is that you can do things now for pennies that would have cost hundreds or thousands of dollars to set up ten years ago.